Standing With God Help

Jeanette Lewis

This is a continue book of the first book "Stop the Crying" which

include love, pain, sorrow, faith and dedication.

Copyright

Copyright © 2026 Jeanette Lewis

Published by

Dedications

Giving all glory and honor to God.

To my mother and father who corrected me when I needed to be corrected growing up.

To my daughter and son that corrects my strong character at times.

To my grandson who permitted me to use his drawing as the cover on this book.

Acknowledgement

I am profoundly grateful to the following people who played pivotal roles in my journey.

First and foremost, to God, who granted me the miracle of surviving brain tumor surgery and inspired the very title of this book.

To my brilliant surgeon, whose steady hands and expertise saved my life, and to the compassionate nurses who cared for me with unwavering kindness during my recovery.

And to my dear friend, who stepped in at a critical moment to help me submit the manuscript to the publisher, turning my dream into reality.

Table of Contents

Chapter 1

It was a chilly December morning on Old Cutler Road. The rain showered around the patio as Janet and Devon huddled close together, both felt so comfortable with the blanket that was snuggling around them. They admired the beauty of the world around them, praising God for its creation, even as they savored the hot chocolate in their hands.

Janet lay in her husband's arms, feeling the familiar safety in his warm embrace. It had been four years since Devon started his path as a minister, having enlisted as an assistant pastor at their local church some time ago. A man of God, steadfast and devoted.

The couple had just celebrated their ten years together in August. They hosted a large dinner at their favorite restaurant, inviting the relatives from both sides of the family alongside a few friends. The highlight of the gathering had been the arrival of the special band Devon had invited to play music during their dinner. As a pastor, Devon had them place red roses on each table.

Janet didn't know why she was still hesitating. It had been several months since her mother passed away, and Devon had been there every step of the way; a guiding light in her darkest days. So, she finally emptied her heart, knowing he'd listen, like he always did.

"My heart was broken," she sighed. "It was as if I had been torn into a million pieces. Many times, I hid my true feelings, I did not want to worry about you and the boys. I would go into our restroom, crying out to God. And on one lonely and desperate day, He heard me. A voice said, "I am here hold on. 'Hold on, I am here.'

"My mind became clear again, and I began praising God for His goodness. Devon, I thank God every day that I have God to hold on to and for having you and the children in my life."

Devon chose to listen in silence. Instead of a reply, he held his wife close and gave her a big kiss. She could ask for nothing more.

She fondly remembered their trip to Las Vegas. Devon had taken her after her mother passed away in September. He felt she needed a break. To make up for their absence, Devon's parents came down to taking care of the boys during their time away.

Upon returning, Devon took charge of their household. He was deeply concerned for Janet's wellbeing and feared she might fall into depression. He made sure Janet went to the gym, got her hair done when needed. They even played tennis together, a game he had taught her, just as he had taught their two sons.

Her thoughts drifted to her sons, especially Marcus. In a way, he was the one who could most relate to her right now. Marcus had been adopted; a fact they had revealed to him when he was twelve years old. They also told him about who his parents were and where he had come from. How his father was black and his mother German. She had died bringing Marcus into the world, leaving him in the care of his father. Marcus had to understand that his father had taken care of him and did not abandon him, until his terrible car accident.

"Your father was a soldier, just like me." Devon told him. "He was a proud man, a proud father. The death of your mother almost broke him, but with faith in God he persevered. He dedicated himself to taking care of you as a single parent. And he continued to do so till the accident. When your father realized he would not survive, he signed the papers for me to be your guardian. At the time I was not married so my parents helped take care of you.

When they revealed everything to Marcus, Devon and Janet worried that they had perhaps made a mistake. They didn't want the truth to estrange their son from them. But thankfully, that did not happen. If anything, Marcus's love for his adoptive parents grew even more, he often expressed pride at being their son.

Janet took another sip of her hot chocolate. The rain around her had started to die down, the clouds gradually thinning to reveal hints of the morning sunlight. Janet looked up to see a faint rainbow marked its colors across the retreating clouds.

Her thoughts inevitably returned to her family. Unlike today, the clouds that gathered over the household with her mother's failing health never really parted. All they could do was to alleviate the symptoms. She and Devon rotated their days to assist Janet's brother Eric in taking care of Mrs. Johnson, their mother. Eric still lived at their parent's house, having retired from teaching two years ago.

The last six months of her mother's life, her brother Daniel came to live at home to help Eric. Summer took leave from her job to stay with her grandmother for a week.

Like all great people, Mrs. Johnson seemed to sense her time coming to an end beforehand, and she made her preparations quietly. Among her final wishes, she summoned son-in-law, Devon, and made a request from him: When the day came, he was to preach at her funeral.

That day did come, far sooner than any would have liked. Devon stood proudly and he spoke at his mother-in-law's celebration.

The funeral of Mrs. Johnson was a celebration of a Godly woman. Her love for the Lord was matched only by her dedication to the people. Friends of the family came all the way from Daytona Beach, and enough flowers were brought to fill up the entire church. The choir song two of Mrs. Johnson's favorite songs. One after another, people came up to speak of their impressions of and time with Mrs. Johnson. When it was his turn, Eric gave his own speech, short yet filled with emotions. Summer read a poem, and Joshua played Near my God to Thee on the piano.

Pastor Cooper then stood, delivering the word of God. He preached from the New King Bible, Acts 3:19 thru 20, urging repenting so that sins could be blotted out.

Janet vividly remembered her mother's love for this chapter. This was her final message to the world; she wanted the living to know that she had repented of her sins before she left.

Devon then shared his reflections on Mrs. Johnson's life. She had loved through much discrimination in her life. Once, she spoke recalled how she could not try on clothes in the store when she was little. Yet later in life she helps raise two little white girls. She was a loving mother who devoted time to her grandchildren, her neighbors and the elderly. A wonderful mother-in-law and a great cook.

Things slowly returned to normal in the two months following Mrs. Johnson's funeral. Of course, the pain of separation still tortured Janet, but she found solace in bringing flowers to her parents' graves once a week.

It was during one quite evening when everyone gathered once again, surrounding Mr. Dickson as he read Mrs. Johnson's will. The task fell very naturally to him, as he had been the family lawyer for years.

Mr. Dickson waited for everyone to arrive before he started reading the letter Mrs. Johnson in his hands. Mrs. Johnson's distinct handwriting was unmistakable.

"Dearest children", Mr. Dickson began, his recitation, "the home that belonged to me and your father is left to all of you. After you all have passed it goes to the grandchildren, if none of the grandchildren care to live there, they can sell and evenly divide the money among themselves evenly.

"Eric may live there for as long as he desires and make no changes to the house unless everyone agrees. You will always make decisions together concerning the home that will always be me and your Dad.

"To each of my beloved children I leave five thousand dollars.

"To my three lovely grandchildren I leave two thousand dollars each.

"To my dearest son-in law, I leave one thousand dollars toward the church that you will be the main pastor one day.

I must say that many people have asked me were you white? I laughed and said are you kidding his mother is black.

"Still, I thank you, Devon, for helping Eric many times as he cared for me. I enjoyed the little trip you and Eric took me on as we went outside to feel the sun. It meant the world to me.

"Janet, you prepared all my favorite meals for me. I thank you, for giving me such comfort. Daniel, thank you for coming to help your brother and keep me company. Grandchildren, thank you for your love and devotion to me.

"I love each one of you very much. Just remember this, I took a long trip to see your father and the kids' grandfather. A permanent vacation we all must take one day.

"I have been the happiest wife, mother, and grandmother in the world. God blessed my life to be good, very good, even when things were hard and difficult at times. During my husband's life, he was my best friend and lover. He honored God deeply. He was a good husband and father. He was also my best friend and lover. He knew in his heart he was the light of my life. Being married to him was amazing and I thank God for the years we shared together. My husband always said ask the Holy Spirit to live through you, so it will shine on your face. That is why I miss him dearly.

"I am so proud that you kids did not worry about my will, just accepting what I had already put in place. God kept my mind sound to the end of my days. Eric took care of me; he never complained. God bless you all for being loving children.

"If you need me, call my name, and I will come. I will be near, you can't see me, but if you listen with your heart, you will feel my love all around you.

"Thanks for the love you showed me, goodbye for now."

By the time Mr. Dickson finished, the entire family was in tears. They gathered their checks, hugged Mr. Dickson and left.

Two weeks after reading Mrs. Johnson's will, Summer left to go back to Manhattan, New York, where she worked as a News Caster. Daniel returned to San Diego California were he lived and worked for Delta airlines as an Air traffic controller.

Chapter 2

The sun had gone down this Friday evening, the weather outside was still cool and pleasant.

Devon had completed all his running around for the day. He made plans to take the family to Key West for a few days before school started again. His thoughts drifted to his older son, Marcus, who would be graduating in June.

As he drove his car close to home, Devon called out to God. "God," he said, "I love you so much. I trust you greatly with my family. I thank you for taking those evil ones out of my son's school—they were calling my sons 'white boys' because of the lightness of their skin and their straight hair. Those kids were so ruled they even asked why their mother's skin was brown. My sons would say, 'She tans very well.' My sons know who they are, and they believe in you, God. They trust you, believing that no weapon formed against them shall prosper. So, I praise you, God, that we got through that. I have taught my sons to say that we are all God children, and every human being bleeds the same red blood. Thank you, Lord, for listening to my prayer. I decided to not let the world invade my very soul. Amen."

Marcus got accepted to the University of San Diego to study engineering. He would be attending there. His uncle Daniel lived in San Diego, so he could visit him sometime.

Marcus told his parents he did not want a car in the first year in college. When he decided, he told his dad he could come there to assist in purchasing the car. Marcus's parents told him that idea was great, and they would take it under great consideration.

After arriving home, Devon yelled out to his wife to meet him in the den before dinner. She arrived in the den, kissing her husband and telling him how much she missed him, even when he went out for just a short period.

"Janet," he said, "let's get the boys ready now so that we can go to Key West." Devon called out to the boys to get ready for dinner. Marcus and Joshua washed up and came to the table to join their parents.

Marcus asked his parents if he could lead the grace for the meal. They nodded, and he asked everyone to bow their heads—they did. "Dear heavenly father," he said, "thank you for the food we are about to eat and for Mom preparing this great meal. May we have a safe trip to Key West, and may the rest of the school year be safe for me, my brother, and all the kids. Amen."

After the meal, Devon instructed the boys to go and pack some clothing in their luggage bags, because in the morning they would be going to Key West for a few days. The boys were so excited they ran to their rooms, while Janet put the dishes in the dishwasher.

Devon whispered in his wife's ear to join him in the den, so that he could have a slow dance with her. He put on that slow song, "A Rainy Night in Georgia." They danced twice before going to their bedroom. Devon checked quickly on the boys, and they had fallen asleep.

The couple made passionate love, took a warm shower, washing one another's body parts. After drying themselves, they prayed together, got into their king-size bed, and fell asleep in each other's arms.

The next morning came earlier than usual. Everyone got their belongings loaded into the car, and the family took off for a few days. The weather was cool in Key West, but the family still enjoyed the beach water.

Devon had decided, with Janet's approval, to send Joshua to a Christian school for his last four years of school. Even though the boys at their school had been put out because of their racist remarks, he felt in his heart—and Janet felt the same—that the change should be made. They prayed about it and felt God had given them the okay to let their son attend a Christian school.

Chapter 3

Marcus Heads to College

Marcus graduated from high school, and the family prepared for a college trip to the University of San Diego so he could start summer classes. He wanted to stay on campus for the first two years.

Devon called the airlines for round-trip tickets, booked a hotel near the college, and arranged a rental car.

The family spent five days with Marcus, helping him settle in and ensuring he had everything needed for the school year.

On their last evening together before flying out the next morning, they shared a nice dinner. Before leaving, the boys hugged each other tightly—the brothers had become very close. Joshua looked up to his big brother, asking all kinds of questions and even requesting to sleep in his room now and then.

Of course, Janet cried on the way back to the hotel. She covered her face a little, not wanting Devon and Joshua to see the tears in her eyes.

In the car, Janet thought for a moment, then spoke: "My darling Devon, we can get Joshua more music classes with the piano, and he says he wants to learn the drums also."

Journey

Back home, they found a Christian school for Joshua that had a school band. They also enrolled him in a music school for the last weeks of summer, where he learned the drums.

He picked it up quickly—the instructor told his parents he had a special gift from God.

Joshua even taught himself the song "I Trust in God," his special song that he played all the time when practicing in his room.

Joshua started his school year at the new school. Of course, Devon took him and picked him up every day.

Devon and Janet continued visiting homeless shelters, doing as much as they could to help improve them. They also took food to feed those in need.

Devon Becomes Head Pastor

Devon preached on the second and third Sundays of each month. One first Sunday, when the pastor announced that Pastor Cooper would be speaking, the church cheered as he walked up to the pulpit.

Before he spoke, Pastor Hard made a special announcement: "I am glad to say today that Pastor Cooper will be the head pastor of this church starting right now. I have prayed about this for a long time. God let me know that it is the right time. For medical reasons, I am stepping down and leaving you with a man of God that I love and respect."

It was silent for a while, then everyone started clapping and praising God. Tears entered Devon's eyes while Janet and Joshua praised God all over the church.

"Now I will let Pastor Cooper speak."

That day, Pastor Cooper spoke to the young people: "Let no one despise you for your youth, but set the believers an example in speech, in conduct, in love, in faith, and in purity" (1 Timothy 4:12).

Twenty young people gave their lives to Christ that day. It was a great day no one would ever forget—young people fell all over the altar, calling out Jesus' name. Pastor Cooper felt in his heart that everything had fallen into place at the right time. On each person, he put praying oil on their forehead.

Church lasted three more hours, no one cared. They just wanted to praise God and sing songs. Finally, after everyone had been anointed and confessed accepting Jesus Christ, Pastor Cooper led the prayer, and church was over.

A Family Promise and a Divine Dream

That night after church, Devon and Janet had a slight disagreement before reaching their bed for sleep. They reminded one another of their promise: the one thing they vowed before marriage—that they would never go to bed without peace among themselves.

The two repeated their apologies to each other before falling asleep that night.

The following night, Devon sat on the edge of the bed, humming and saying, "Yes Lord." His humming woke Janet up. She immediately called out, "Devon! Is anything wrong?"

He answered, "Nothing, my love. I just had a dream telling me to keep preaching the gospel—do not get discouraged. The Holy Spirit reminded me to always be thankful and keep the faith. I want those words to always flow from my heart and lips. I know being patient will draw me even closer to our loving God. Now, my dearest wife, I can go back to sleep."

He slowly got back under the covers and fell asleep.

Church Growth Under New Leadership

The following Sunday, the church welcomed Pastor Cooper and his wife as the new pastor and first lady.

Pastor Hard and the members surprised Pastor Cooper and his wife with a celebration in the hall after church, welcoming them into their positions.

After settling into his new position for three months, Pastor Cooper made a few changes: he chose his two assistant pastors, kept the same deacons, and left the choir members the same. Joshua, their son, joined the music group as the second piano player.

His wife organized a new group for women fifty and over. The group met twice a month and went on free group lunches every six months. She made sure someone remained over the teen ministry, teaching the younger kids and teens during church time.

There was a team that gathered once a month to feed people at the homeless shelter. The pastor met with the assistant pastors and deacons once a month, with lunch served to them.

Within six months, the church had 500 new members. The church was growing, and more people became volunteers for children's church and teen church.

The church was only open three days a week for prayer and administrative work.

Chapter 4

A Quiet Friday Evening Turns Somber

A quiet Friday evening, the family retired early.

The phone rang. Devon answered calmly: "Hello, this is the Cooper residence. How can I help you?"

A lady's low voice spoke: "This is the nursing home where Uncle Joe is."

"Oh yes," Devon answered. "How is Uncle Joe?"

The lady said, "I am Helen, the supervisor on duty this morning. Sorry to inform you that Uncle Joe passed in his sleep last night. We went to his room after he did not come to breakfast—he was lying in bed like he was sleeping. The doctors checked him, and the report from the hospital said it was natural death; he was just old."

Devon told Helen they would be there in a few days. As soon as he hung up, he gave Janet the news. They cried together. That night, they fell asleep holding one another tightly.

Devon said, "My love, we have gone through a few tragedies these past years, but we are still standing with God strength."

Preparing for the Trip

Janet decided to write Summer and Marcus a letter informing them about Uncle Joe's death. She did not want to upset Marcus during the midterms testing. As fair as Summer, she is in New York without family.

When morning came, Devon made a simple breakfast for the three of them: hashbrowns, scrambled eggs, toast, and orange juice. Joshua said grace, giving honor to God and thanking Him for the food they were about to eat. He thanked God for having Uncle Joe in their lives and prayed for the family to have a safe trip.

After the meal, Devon addressed the issue: they had to travel to Daytona Beach for Uncle Joe's burial. Joshua went to his room to practice his music.

Janet and Devon decided to take a warm, steaming shower together, washing each other's hair and bodies. This relaxed their minds and bodies.

They lay on the bed together after the shower. Devon held Janet close, speaking in a low voice: "Janet, his death is so unexpected, but Uncle Joe had all his papers together. I have them in our safe. He never wanted to bother you—he said you made sure he was taken care of after Douglas died, and he was so grateful."

Travel and Final Arrangements

The next two days, Devon called Delta Airlines to confirm round-trip tickets and a rental car upon arrival in Daytona Beach. Janet packed her and Devon's clothing and made sure Joshua had the proper items in his luggage.

The third day, Eric took them to the airport for the trip to Daytona Beach. They stayed in the home they still had there.

Devon settled Joshua and Janet in the home, then left for the nursing home.

After arriving, he asked to see Uncle Joe's room. He walked in slowly, head bent down for a few minutes, thinking of how happy Uncle Joe had been when he, Janet, and Joshua made that special visit on his birthday. A sadness came upon his face when he saw a picture of Uncle Joe with Marcus and Joshua, and another of him and the entire family on the desk.

Devon packed the rest of Uncle Joe's clothing, shoes, and other items. He closed out all the paperwork and signed Uncle Joe out.

He went by the funeral home where the small service would be held. He took them the brown suit Uncle Joe wanted to be dressed in, along with matching shoes and socks, and all other items needed for the occasion. He chose a gray casket and bought the flower arrangement for it. Devon invited the few people who still remembered Uncle Joe, plus all the seniors from the nursing home would attend.

The Funeral Service

Uncle Joe's service was held on a Saturday morning in the funeral home with all those who loved and remembered him.

Devon spoke from the King James Bible, Joshua chapter 24, verses 14 to 30, which speaks of fearing the Lord and serving Him in sincerity and truth.

After the service, Devon and his family, along with a few other people, followed the funeral car to the same gravesite where Douglas's body was. Uncle Joe had requested to be put next to Douglas; Devon made sure that happened.

Devon spoke the last words when the casket was put in the ground: "Dust to dust and ashes to ashes." Joshua and Janet held each other and cried together as they left the gravesite.

The family spent three more days in their home, then caught a flight back to Miami.

Chapter 5

Welcome Home and Family Plans

Eric was at the airport when they arrived that Wednesday evening. He met them in the luggage claim to help with their luggage. They hugged one another, then went to Eric's car.

Eric started speaking: "I prepared a meal for you, so before I take you home, we'll go by Mama Johnson's home and eat."

Everyone thanked him, especially Joshua: "Uncle Eric, I am starving now!" Everyone began laughing.

Janet said, "My dearest family, we must go back to what Mom wanted us to continue—having dinner in her home after church."

"Okay," Eric said. "We'll start this Sunday. We go to her grave after church service, then to our parents' home to eat."

Devon said, "That's great, and I agree totally. This Sunday, I have the honor of a guest speaker, Pastor Moss from Jamaica. I'm sure those from Jamaica will be pleased."

Sunday Morning Church Service

When Sunday morning came, it was sunny outside. Janet got up and prepared a breakfast Devon would very much enjoy: ginger tea, veggie eggs, wheat toast, turkey sausage, plus apple juice. For her and Joshua, they had scrambled white eggs, turkey sausage, and orange juice.

Janet completed the meal and called everyone to the table, where Devon said grace.

They finished in time to get ready for church. Devon put the dishes in the dishwasher.

This Sunday, the church was packed—many people came as usual. After the announcements, Pastor Cooper stepped up to the pulpit to introduce the guest, Pastor Moss from Jamaica. He preached from Psalm 29:2: "Give unto the Lord the glory due unto his name; worship the Lord in the beauty of holiness."

The congregation began praising the Lord and worshipping Him all over the church. Many called out God name, and many started repenting, asking God into their lives.

For those who wanted to repent and be saved, Pastor Moss called them to the front, anointed them with oil, and asked them to repeat the sinner's prayer. He welcomed them to the house of the Lord and to being born again.

He spoke about being open to thoughts of God and His goodness: "Allow your imagination to paint a picture of great possibilities in your lives. Amen." And church was over.

Lunch and Farewell

After church, Pastor Cooper, Mrs. Cooper, and Joshua took Pastor Moss to lunch at a steak house. Before he came into town, they spoke to his church, which informed them he enjoyed a good steak.

When they got to a table, Pastor Cooper presented Pastor Moss with a love offering from him and the first lady. "I did not want to ask the congregation for an offering—some families are going through hard times, and the church is helping them out. The first lady and I are doing fine, so we can give you love offerings out of our own savings."

After lunch, they drove Pastor Moss to American Airlines, where they said a prayer together before he caught his flight back home.

Chapter 6

Church Improvements and Gratitude

Two months after the guest speaker had come and gone, Pastor Cooper got new seats in the church, new carpet throughout, plus new tile for certain areas.

The pastor also announced that the mortgage on the church had been paid off—the church now owned the property. "You see, I spoke about tithes and offerings, but I did not repeat it too many times during my sermons. I knew God would touch your hearts, and you gave freely."

Everyone stood up and began praising God and giving thanks to Almighty God.

"I would like to give special thanks to Ms. Woods, the treasurer, and the first lady, for keeping the funds intact. After this service, there will be punch and cake served in the back."

Janet's Headache and Diagnosis

One night after Joshua had gone to bed, Janet and Devon relaxed in the den for a few hours, the weeks had been so busy for them.

Janet began telling Devon that the front of her head was hurting. "I forgot to tell you—I hit my head on the trunk of my car."

"My love," he said, "we will go to the emergency room after I drop off Joshua in the morning."

Janet rose extra early that morning and made a small breakfast for the three of them: pancakes, veggie eggs, turkey bacon, and orange juice.

They let Joshua say grace that morning. The three got in the car after Devon put the dishes in the dishwasher.

After dropping him off, they headed to the emergency room at Baptist Hospital. They explained the problem and waited. They took an MRI, which detected a tumor on the brain.

The doctor said, "It does not look like cancer, but it must be removed before it gets any larger. We would have to go through her nose on the right side."

Janet and Devon prayed together for twenty minutes, then gave the doctor the okay.

Preparing for Surgery

The surgery was scheduled for a Friday two weeks from the appointment—a day when teachers had a workday off and school was closed.

Devon took Janet home to rest while he picked up Joshua from school. On the way home, he said, "My dearest son, your mom must have surgery on her head—there is a tumor on her brain; it must be removed."

Joshua started crying. "Dad, will Mom die like Grandmom and Uncle Joe?"

"No, this is not that serious, and God has this under control. We are family—God has put us together for a long time to come."

After arriving home, Joshua ran in the house calling out, "Mom! Mom, where are you?"

"Joshua!" she yelled. "I am in the den!"

He ran to the den. "Mom, I love you! I heard about your problem."

"Calm down, my son—everything will be okay. They found the problem in time, and now they will remove it. Remember, we trust in God; He is the healer."

Devon came in and told them he was going out to get dinner. "What would you like?"

Janet said, "Chicken." They all agreed. Devon left to purchase their meal.

While Devon was out purchasing dinner, Joshua took a shower and dressed for bed. On Devon's return, Janet said grace before dinner. She spoke about giving gratitude to the great God, not only for the food that they were about to eat, but for his Greatness and how she depends on him. "That is why I see miracles", she said. "I communicate with you, God, because I want your thoughts in my mind…I want you to guide my feet along with my family, as long as we live. Amen."

Chapter 7

Janet's Surgery Day

The weeks passed. Devon and Janet decided not to inform Marcus and Summer until everything was over.

Devon only spoke to his administrative staff, who came in three days a week to work around the property. The doors were always open for prayer.

The day of the surgery, it was warm outside, and the sky was blue—no dark clouds at all. It was a beautiful day that the Lord had made. They reported to the hospital at 6:30 a.m.; surgery was at 10:00 a.m.

Devon and Joshua prayed with Janet before they took her in for the operation.

Four hours passed. The doctor came out and spoke to Devon: "Everything went well, you can see her soon."

"God bless you, Doctor Bill, and thanks for catching that problem in time. Most of all, I give God all the glory for giving you the proper knowledge and blessing your hands that did the work."

Recovery and Family Support

Within the three days, Janet received so many flowers that she gave some to patients who had none.

After arriving home, Devon contacted his son and daughter, letting them speak to their mom and wish her a great recovery.

Then Devon contacted his parents, letting them speak to Janet. They wished her well, saying if she needed them, they would come. She told them Devon and a few church members had everything under control.

An Unexpected Visitor

One evening, Devon was in his office when suddenly he looked up—a lady was standing in his door. He asked, "Did you come for prayer?"

She answered loudly, "No, I come for you, Pastor."

"What do you mean?" he said in a confused voice.

"I heard your wife is sick. Then I heard a voice telling me that you need my help—that you need a woman till your wife gets well."

The pastor said, "God did not tell me that, so I would like for you to leave now. My wife, the first lady of this church, is the only woman I need. I am dedicated to her, my respect is for her, and I don't want to live in this world without her."

Pastor Cooper pushed the alarm button under his desk. One of the assistant pastors came to his office. "Pastor, is there a problem?"

"Yes, Pastor Allen," he said calmly. "The young lady seems to have a problem—she is saying God told her that I need her because my wife is sick."

Pastor Allen turned to the young woman with a smile. "I am here to escort you out of this office. If you care for prayer, we will pray at the altar before you leave."

The young lady agreed. They walked to the altar; Pastor Allen prayed with her, then escorted her outside, waited till she got in her car, and drove away.

Safeguards and Reflection

Devon decided to get a buzzer on the church door that day. No longer would the doors be unlocked for individuals to freely walk in.

After picking up Joshua that day, he stopped and bought Janet a dozen roses and her favorite chocolate candy.

When arriving home that evening, he discussed the situation with his wife. They prayed with one another; Devon asked God to help the young lady find her way.

Devon and Janet sat on their patio that night, looking at the moon and a few stars. They remembered what they had been through in their life: the great times, the times of sadness, the pain, and even the sorrow they had experienced.

"No matter what has happened," they said to one another, "we are standing with God help."

Full Recovery and Lessons Learned

Janet recovered and returned to church as the first lady.

Someone sent a letter to the church explaining that the young lady who appeared that day had mental illness and was getting treatment.

The pastor decided to have professionals come in to talk to the members about how to recognize mental illness and handle different situations. "May God bless and keep us all. We must always welcome these words: God is all around us—His love, His wisdom, His peace, and protection forever."

This is why we must live by faith, not by sight. I encourage you to rejoice and be glad as you walk through each day. Deep in my heart, I believe God does his greatest work through those with grateful and trusting hearts.

Chapter 8

A Shooting at the Church

Several months have passed since the incident at the church. More people had become members.

A windy Wednesday morning, after Devon dropped off Joshua at school, he decided to go by the church to make sure the outside cameras were working.

He got out of his car, walked slowly up to the church door, and heard a loud sound like a gun. He dropped to the sidewalk right there in front of the church.

He quickly turned his body around and witnessed a woman running toward the street.

He checked his body for gunshot wounds but had none. He then called 911 and explained what had happened. In no time, there were four patrol cars on the scene and an ambulance.

His church had become a crime scene. The bullet was found in the front door; the camera caught the woman clearly—her face was clear.

The pastor told them she had come to the church several months back, seeking him, saying God said she should be with him.

All reports were taken. Devon explained he had to call his wife, he knew she would be wondering what had happened. He also told the officers he would go to the doctor after speaking to her.

Prayer and Assurance to the Congregation

Members from the church had gathered in front to pray and ask to speak to Pastor Cooper.

Before leaving the scene, Pastor Cooper stood in front of the crowd: "Thank you for your great concern, but you must go back to your homes. The church will be closed for a few weeks, but I will hold service in the parking lot at 11 a.m. on Sunday till the doors are open again."

Everyone cheered him on and wished him well.

Homecoming and News Coverage

Pastor Cooper got in his car and drove slowly home, with all the thoughts of what had taken place a few hours ago.

He arrived home to neighbors and so many people standing in his yard, along with reporters.

He spoke up in front of one reporter before opening his house door: "I do not have much to say at this time, except Almighty God spared my life today. I am so grateful. I owe my very life to our amazing and wonderful God, forever. I have to stay conscious of God even when I go through this day. Believing and knowing he will never leave my side. I will let the Holy Spirit guide me step by step, protecting me all the way." The crowd started clapping. Devon turned around and headed for his front door.

Janet opened the door, gave her husband a big kiss and a warm hug. "Neighbors and church members have been bringing food all morning and having prayer with me. My wonderful husband, the church has been all over the news. Some newscasters were saying the Man of God, head of the

Church of Deliverance, was almost murdered by a woman who longed for his company."

The news flashed the woman's picture all over, requesting she give herself up.

They talked for hours and prayed for hours, giving thanks to the Lord God who protected him that very day.

Family Reunion and Forgiveness

Devon finally looked at his watch: "Janet, it is time to pick up Joshua."

"Love," she said, "I will ride with you today—we need that closeness at this time."

When Joshua got in the car, he said: "I heard about the situation at the church. My teacher allowed us to have a moment of silent prayer."

All the way home, Janet and Joshua kept the conversation going about what had happened that day.

Arriving home, everyone washed up for dinner. Janet said a long, heart-warming grace. At the meal's end, Devon placed the dishes in the washer.

Devon gathered everyone in the den: "I am calling Marcus and Summer now so we can all talk together."

The call took place that night. Janet and Devon explained to the two children what had happened early that morning. Before hanging up, Devon told his family, "For my heart and mind to be right, I have to forgive this lady."

His kids and wife said they would forgive also.

Devon led the prayer, said goodnight, and hung up. Joshua said goodnight to his parents and went to bed.

Call to Parents and Rest

Before they retired from bed, Devon had to call his parents. When his father answered, he took his time speaking.

"Sorry, Dad," Devon said. "Janet and I had to call to let you and Mom know about what took place today."

He began explaining what happened that morning. His dad said, "Oh my God. This goes to show God is with you. Most of all, you are safe, and we must give Him glory. I will tell your mom in the morning—let's not wake her at this time."

"Okay, Dad. I love you, and we will talk later." Devon hung up with a smile and great relief.

The two of them went to bed that night, kissing and holding each other tight till both fell asleep.

Chapter 9

Justice Served

Early that morning, Devon turned on the television to breaking news: the woman who tried to murder the pastor of the Church of Deliverance had been caught and was in custody.

"That was good news," he told Janet and Joshua while eating breakfast.

Weeks went by. A trial was held; the woman was found guilty of attempted murder. She was sentenced to six years in prison.

Pastor Cooper spoke at the sentencing: "I ask the judge to make sure she gets mental health help while serving her time in jail." In his heart, he thought of forgiveness—not just for her, but for the healing it brought his family.

End of School Year and Family Trip Plans

It was the end of the school year. Summer took leave from her job for a month; Marcus did not attend summer school that summer.

Daniel took leave for a month from his job.

Devon's parents came down to visit for a month. They decided to take the entire family to Italy for four weeks, all expenses paid by them.

His father said, "My wife and I have this money; why not enjoy it with the ones we love?" Devon smiled inwardly, grateful for parents who turned savings into shared joy.

Daniel and Summer slept over at their grandmother's house with Eric till they left for the trip. Eric and Daniel made dinner for the family on Sundays till they left.

Cherished Family Moments

Devon would play tennis with his wife and kids on Saturdays, taking those walks in the neighborhood, and bringing the family to the homeless shelter to do work. These simple routines, he reflected, wove their lives tighter, a quiet strength amid trials.

Final Sermon Before the Trip

The Sunday before they left for the trip, Pastor Cooper gave his sermon on peace, love, and forgiveness.

He reminded his congregation: "As long as the Church of Deliverance stands, I will preach about God's great love, His forgiveness, His compassion. May our hearts stay close to Him and our faith continue to grow. Let the light of His love fill us. Remember, God's love is that everlasting love."

His Eye is on The Sparrow

"To my Black Mother, Daughter and Every Black woman. My respect and honor go out to you, for remaining standing in what you believe in, no matter what society has thrown towards you."

Let us all remember that one act of kindness can change someone's life

Me and my family remain standing with God help.

I have entrusted my entire life to my Lord and savior Jesus Christ.

Eye Sketch Drawn by my granddaughter: Oceious Thorpe